The Art of Presales

Workbook

The Art of Presales Workbook, 2nd Edition.

ISBN: 9798793779708

Written and illustrated by Dr Tuuli Bell

Foreword by Aaron Davies

Publisher: Tuuli Bell Ltd

https://www.tuulibell.com/

Praise for the first edition

"This is an excellent workbook -- Thought-provoking quotations appear throughout and the reader is encouraged to "fill-in-the-blanks" as they go, making use of the visual guides and diagrams contained within."

"I bought your workbook to understand how I can do presales better, but what I love about it which is something I've been looking for is some means of getting my longer term game plan in better shape. -- The big mistake I think I made is not having a meaningful long term game plan to set out what I need to accomplish, both work and personal. So... trying to be brutally honest with myself and using your workbook to help lay this out."

For David,
thank you for your love & support over the years.
Tuuli x

v

Welcome
to

your
future

This book belongs to:

_____

Foreword by Aaron Davies

I have recruited for a lot of start-ups over the years. Some of them went on to become true unicorns, some fizzled out and others simply got their execution all wrong.

Regardless of each individual story, all of these tech companies had one thing in common: they were all in need of high calibre sales engineering talent. Such is the importance of getting the right people in place, pretty much every CEO recognised that it could make or break the success of their company. Within a tech company, the pre-sales engineer is rather like a swiss army knife who sits at the intersection of technical knowledge, commercial nous and an ability to simultaneously understand how the magic fits together whilst appreciating the business value and proposition. The most successful amongst them have an innate ability to position and to persuade - you could say that their multifaceted talents are borderline mercurial and yet, there are many who dismiss them simply as salespeople with an above average of the technical components.

To categorise them as such is to completely misunderstand the value they bring to the organisation. It is a rare salesperson who can go through the (often complex) sales process and successfully close a major deal without the help of an accomplished sales engineer by their side.

Their task is not to be confused with those on the "post sales" side of the fence. Those folks tend to be more oriented toward implementation, architectural scoping, training and on-boarding to give a few typical examples.

Crucially, they are not considered to be the ones involved in closing the sale itself. Post sales professionals tend to enter the scene after the deal is signed.

Given their versatility, presales engineers are often accustomed to wearing many different hats, working across different departments and as a result, are frequently expected to travel extensively. Not only are they highly technically skilled, they tend to be commercially savvy and sales oriented, which is why they often work closely with sales professionals and undertake tasks such as completing RFPs, providing demos and running POCs. Remuneration is commonly calculated on a 80/20 split (sometimes 70/30) and their commission payments are often tied to revenue.

Having recruited for presales professionals for over 15 years, I have had the privilege of working with some truly outstanding professionals, regarded as subject matter experts in their field. Frequently, I have been tasked with sourcing candidates that needed to possess an exceptionally wide and diverse range of skills and experience.

The best sales engineers have been those who have demonstrated the 'full package' i.e. those who had worked in a wide range of company environments (both start-up and corporate,) been through acquisitions, IPOs, perhaps launched their own businesses. In other words, they carried "battle scars" and had been there, done that, got the T-shirt, to borrow a common expression. They were often polished, knowledgeable, cool under pressure and quick to learn.

Most importantly, those who remained humble despite earning the right perhaps to be very confident in their abilities, were the most impressive among them. They tended to be the individuals who strove to help others and to lead by example.

So, let's imagine two scenarios. In the first case, let's assume that you are an established presales engineer who is seeking to make their next career move. Unless you are following a former boss into your next role, it is quite likely that you will encounter recruiters and/or hiring managers along the interview process.

What skills do these individuals tend to look for and how do you convey them through a resume/CV before having the chance to interact with that person? Whilst each stakeholder in the process will hold their own views, quirks and preferences based on their own particular pain point, the overall composition of abilities doesn't generally differ within the sales engineering organisation. Domain experience, seniority level and location are more likely to be the components which change rather than target personality.

I can only speak with any authority on hiring for the technology/software industry, but the principles remain the same. To be sufficiently attractive to potential employers, there must be the same fundamentally compelling reasons in place for wanting to engage with or reach out to that presales consultant. Generally speaking, they should possess intellectual curiosity (for how things work, how a value proposition solves problems and/or provides a ROI) mental horsepower, adaptability and a nuanced balance of technical proficiency and commercial awareness. An experienced practitioner may be given the opportunity to serve as a "first on the ground" employee, charged with establishing operations in a new territory, travelling extensively to meet and onboard customers, which in itself calls for a whole host of additional attributes such as initiative, self-motivation and ambition.

For an individual who is seeking to make a move into presales, there are other considerations involved. It's fair to say that most people will find it easier to transition into a presales role within their current organisation than to try and seek their first role in presales in a new company. This is not a hard and fast rule, but in the experience of this writer a greater rate of success is assured by making the move whilst in-situ.

Some of the most successful presales engineers have made their way from disciplines such as technical support, technical account management and of course, sales itself.

Whatever path you choose, I can wholeheartedly recommend striving for a career in presales. It is a highly rewarding position within a technology business, not without hard work and challenges but the rewards are very much on offer for those at the top of their profession. You will be seen as the go-to subject matter expert, you will be asked to speak at tech conferences, run demos, answer a never-ending stream of questions, to think on your feet and come up with creative solutions to tough business problems. Notwithstanding the many expectations heaped upon your shoulders, you will earn well, travel the world and earn the deep respect of your colleagues and customers. Get ready for the ride - I wish you all the best of luck!

- Aaron Davies, Executive Headhunter, Jurupa

How to use this workbook

The perfect antidote to those many hours working on your laptop, there's something calming about putting your thoughts on a piece of paper. This journal is designed for you to take time off your day, sit back and reflect on what is meaningful to you, at work and otherwise. It's also a great excuse to take out those coloured pencils and do some doodling whilst thinking deep thoughts.

Those who know me, will attest to the fact that I can find routines difficult. By nature, I like to feel free of constraints and heavy structures. I have found the hard way that routines can be a powerfully positive way to change ourselves and the world around us. Making a conscious decision to work on a specific goal regularly, makes change happen.

Thus, I would encourage you to pick a day of the week now. Promise yourself to dedicate 30 minutes on self-reflection and improvement, every week.

You can explore the workbook from the beginning to the end, or in your chosen order. If you complete a full double page every week, it'll take 18 weeks (a quarter and a half) to achieve full 'presales champion' status.

Who said self-reflection should mean sweat, tears and futuristic plain-colour jumpsuits? I can't promise no tears, but otherwise, make yourself comfortable during your special day. Wear your favourite clothes (I do love jumpsuits by the way), listen to inspiring music or hide away from others. Whatever makes you happy.

If you ever get stuck or need help with any of the exercises, please get in touch with me directly (fan mail also welcome): tuuli.bell@ tuulibell.com. I'll be happy to hear from you.

my day of
reflection:

MON TUE

WED THU

FRI SAT SUN

Becoming a team of champions

Are you an ambitious team of presales consultants? Form your own 'accountability club', asking your named buddy to check up on your progress. Pay back the favour and ensure that your buddy keeps up their good work, too. Schedule a catch up every week. Sometimes, it could be a simple '-done yours?' '- thumbs up' instant message. Other times, you might want to discuss your thoughts in more details. That's fine. Respect each other's feelings and thoughts.

Your journal should remain your journal, and no-one else's. You're welcome to share your journal entries if you want, but don't feel any pressure to do so. The most important thing is that you take the time to yourself.

And when it's time to celebrate, why not do it in style? Give it 20 weeks (we're human in the end - and you'll need a week to find the right outfit) and find a date in your diary for a graduation party!

Accountability club name:

_____

My accountability buddy:

_____

My catch up day and time:

_____

Presales champion graduation party:

_____

"Champions keep playing until they get it right."

- Billie Jean King

What's in the book...

...book contents continued...

me and my vision

My very own vision

Welcome to your very own workbook! I am here to support you on your transformative presales journey. To start off, we'll talk about you: your vision and mission. Don't worry if it's the first time you're doing this exploration, or if you've done it a million times before. It's always refreshing, and very grounding, to write down what you want in life. Vision talks about what you want to achieve in life. What's important to you? What makes you the special 'you'? Use the wheel below, working from the outer circle (environment), through the middle (external factors), to the innermost question.

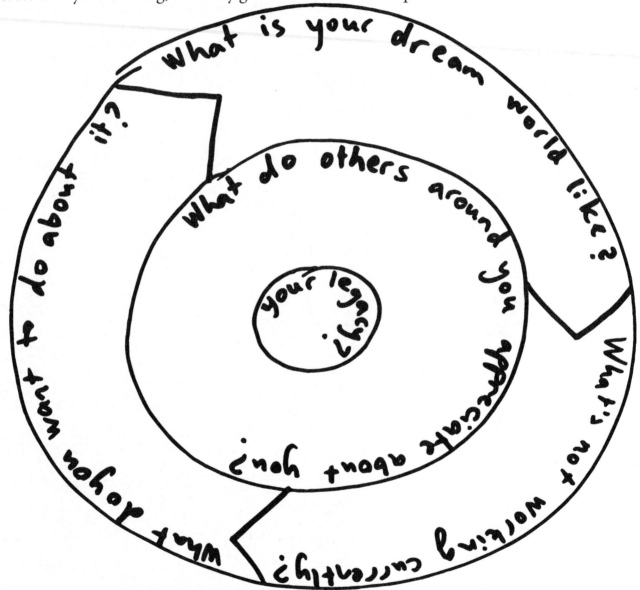

Next, try to summarise your role in creating your dream world, guided by the above.

My vision in life is to

_____

My mission statement

Your mission statement tells you, and others around you, how you achieve your vision. The more specific the statement, the better and more effective it is. Whereas vision rarely changes, your mission statement may alter from time to time as you grow and develop as a person, and as you come into contact with more people and ideas. For example, if your vision is "to create a more peaceful society", your mission could be: "I help local school children aged 4-11 by teaching families empathy skills in an after school club to create a more peaceful society."

My mission statement

"If you don't like the road you're walking, start paving a new one."

-Dolly Parton

Where do I want to be?

What are your main goals for the next 1, 3, or 5 years? Pick your favourite ones, and visualise where you want to be one month from now. Then, break down the goal into sub-actions and sub-goals. Repeat for each main goal, and then... prioritise. Chances are you'll have time to work on 1 or 2 goals every week. Finally, it is time to dream, properly. Use the space on the right to write, draw, or attach pictures of your dream life. What do you want from health, financial wealth, professional/academic growth, relationships and spiritual development?

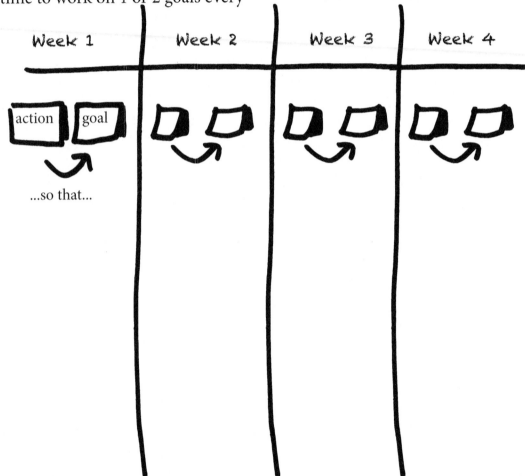

If you're into metrics and trackers, you can add a level of complexity. For each goal, ask yourself: "What will I track my progress with?" or "How will I know I've been succesful?"

My vision board

"If you focus upon whatever you want, you will attract whatever you want. If you focus upon the lack of whatever you want, you will attract more lack."

- Esther and Jerry Hicks, Teachings of Abraham

Causes I care about

Discovering what you really care about, and what is important to you, can be lots of fun. Trust me. By getting curious about the world and finding your passion, what makes you click, is both rewarding and fulfilling. Get inspiration from the list below or add your own.

A fast 'litmus-test' of your passions is to think back to the time you were a five-year old child. What did you enjoy doing? What did you think was most important in life? Even negative memories can display deeper messages and ultimately carry positive meanings.

climate change

technology

gender equality

children's rights

nature

health

peace

diversity

What did I enjoy as a 5-year old?

As a 5-year-old, I really enjoyed…

"Justice is about making sure that being polite is not the same thing as being quiet. In fact, often times, the most righteous thing you can do is shake the table."

- Alexandria Ocasio-Cortez

my current role

My values...

Welcome to the second part of your journey! In this section, we'll discover the congruity between you and your employer. If you work for yourself, are a student, or just not sure who your 'employer' is, this is a great opportunity to assess a future employer's suitability for you. We're going to start with the very basics: what your and your employer's values are. Google will be your best friend here. Every company publishes their values on their website. Try quoting the corporate values to your customers: it creates a deeper connection.

... and my company's values

How well are your personal
values reflected in your work?

"Passion is energy. Feel the power that comes from focusing on what excites you."
- Oprah Winfrey, Media Executive and Philanthropist

Value proposition: the story

As a presales consultant, you are repeating the 'value proposition' to your customers in each interaction. It's the story of your company, the reason why it (still) exists and why customers need to work with you. Stories are a powerful method of communication. Stories make difficult concepts easier to under-stand, and to remember. On this page, write down the 'value proposition' as you've been taught it in corporate presentations. Then, re-write in your own words on the opposite page. Read it out loud and repeat until the words feel your own.

Value proposition in my own words

write it down...

... then read it out loud...
(what worked? what needs changed?)

...write it down again...

... read out loud (try to ig-
nore people around you)...
(still too many buzzwords? are you only
answering 'what' and 'how', but not
'why'?)

...write it down once more...

...can a 10-year-old under-
stand it?

"Tell me the facts and I'll learn. Tell me the truth and I'll believe.
But tell me a story and it will live in my heart forever."

- An old Native American proverb

Typical customer pain points our solution helps solve

Selling is ultimately about understanding what your customers needs (or what they want, or think they need). There's a saying about 'painkillers' vs. 'vitamins' in sales. People will be quite happy to pay for something that takes away a pain ('painkiller') but not necessarily pay to improve things that are already working to an extent ('vitamin').

On this page, try to identify the main pains a customer feels, and then describe how your product or service helps address the specific issues.

Pains
What are the customer pains you help solve?

Gains
How does your product or service ease the pain?

Customer case studies & war stories

Collect your favourite customer stories here. How do your customers benefit from using your company's services and products? What issues did they have, and how where they resolved? Why did you choose that story to be celebrated as one of your favourites?

"I like to say it's an attitude of not just thinking outside the box, but not even seeing the box."

- Safra A. Catz

Standards, frameworks and best practices

Industry standards, frameworks and best practices are designed to make things easier for everybody. However, the mere amount of available frameworks can make you feel put-off by them. Additionally, certain frameworks have a tendency to attract a lot of negative press from 'go-getters' who want to get things done.

When adopted effectively, best practices and other frameworks can be really useful by sharing collective, tacit knowledge. I would encourage you to explore them in more detail and document your findings here.

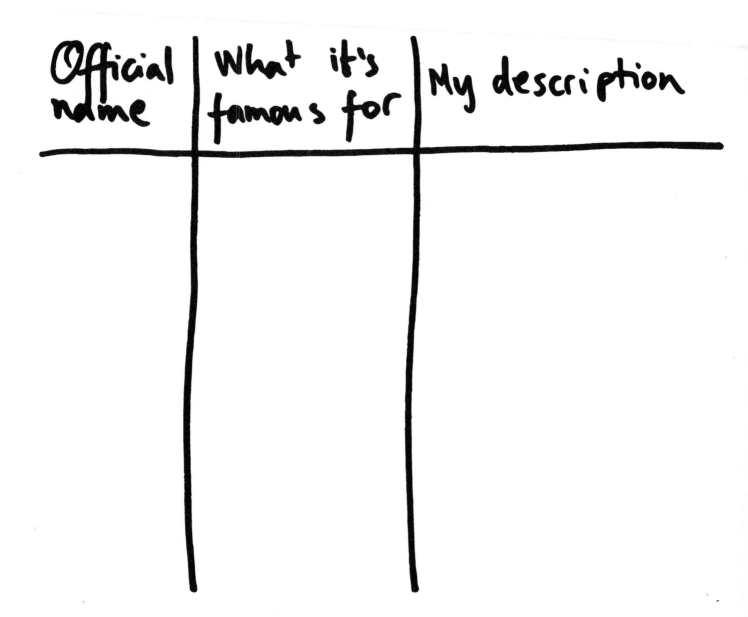

Official name	What it's famous for	My description

My analysis of the frameworks

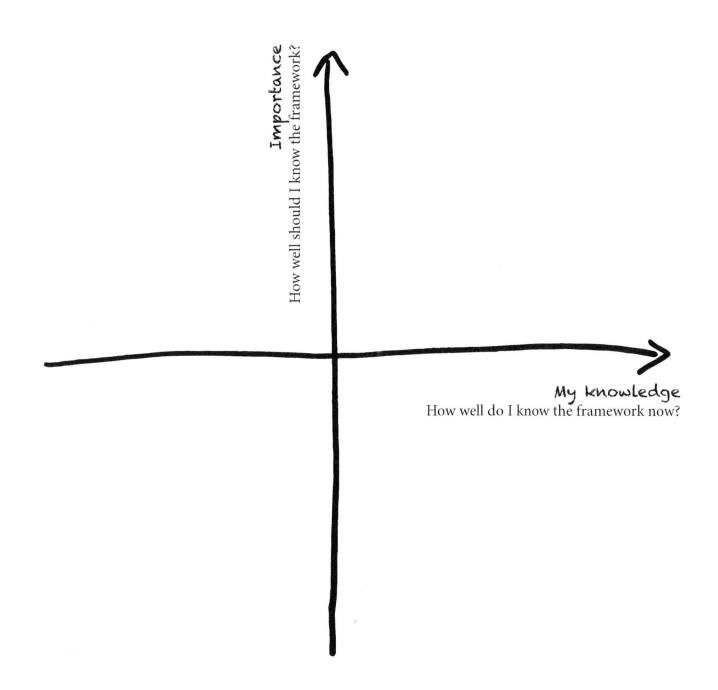

Importance
How well should I know the framework?

My knowledge
How well do I know the framework now?

"Life is a series of building, testing, changing and iterating."
- Lauren Mosenthal, Chief Technology Officer at Glassbreakers

Standard demo flow

Yes, no demo is the same. BUT, a demo always tells a story. That story is based on your company's value proposition, altered only slightly to mirror the words and worlds of the customer. The more demo's you do, the easier they become. At the same time, it can be harder to bring something fresh to a conversation every time. What helped me was to keep a list of mini-stories that highlighted something important about the product, stories that covered typical requirements, and reminders about qualification questions to ask.

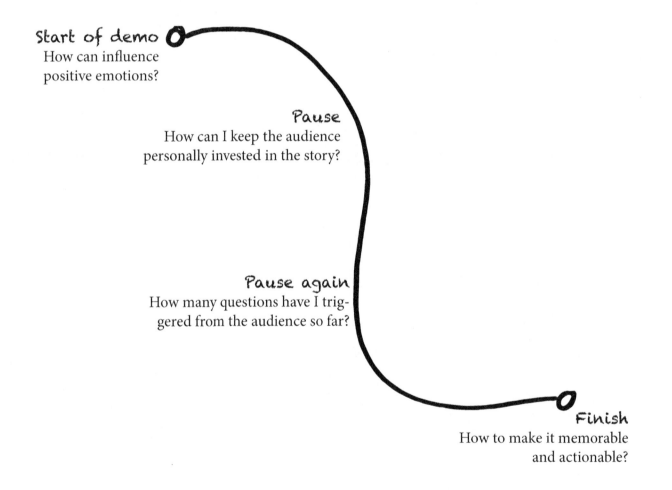

Start of demo
How can influence positive emotions?

Pause
How can I keep the audience personally invested in the story?

Pause again
How many questions have I triggered from the audience so far?

Finish
How to make it memorable and actionable?

Legend

✳	Important
↗	Requirement
?	Question to ask

Let's get practical: a demo flow for a specific customer (past or present)

Customer's code name:

_____

Demo flow:

"The most courageous act is still to think for yourself. Aloud"

- Coco Chanel

Requirements gathering

Gathering requirements is detective work. Unearthing different requirement types including functional, integration, process, process interface, usability, user experience, language, security, and organisational change is not for the faint-hearted. Discovering hidden requirements makes the life of post-sale consultants much easier, and you'll be thanked for your integrity!

Requirements by type

List the important but oft-forgotten requirements on this page, adding more requirement types if necessary. Draw or write the "easier-to-capture" functional requirements on the opposite page.

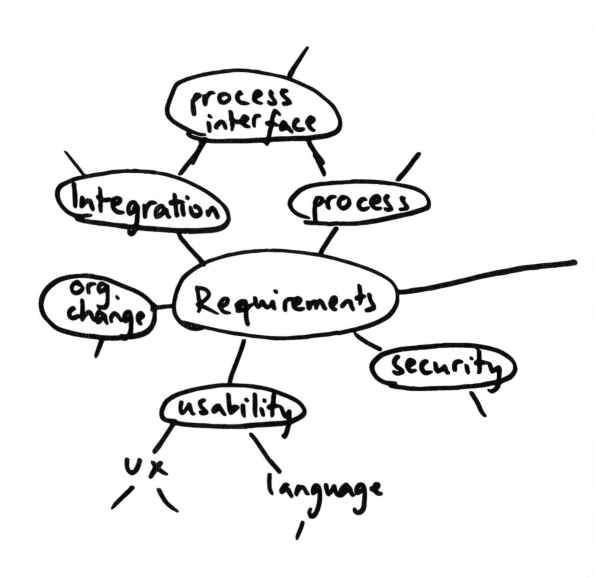

"Knowing what must be done does away with fear."

- Rosa Parks

Solution architecture

The final technical challenge is to take a step back, and draw how your solution fits into a customer environment. Keep the diagram at a high level, drawing your solution in the centre with its integrations to other systems around it. You may consider drawing a circle representing a customer's 'secure network' and placing components in relation to it. If you have a SaaS solution, feel free to draw fluffy clouds and a rainbow to add some colour. (Just maybe remove the rainbow from any formal customer proposals.)

Other diagrams

The information flow within a system is what makes the system, the system. To appreciate how and where the data moves, let's zoom into the solution. Pick you favourite use case scenario, and imagine being a tiny byte of data traversing through the automated processes. For example, if you collect, analyse, transform and communicate data about food eaten by Slender-Snouted Crocodiles in Zoos across the UK, you might imagine the byte's trip from the zoo-keeper to the system, into dashboards to boardrooms.

"Understanding the make up of our environment and our purpose within it, is necessary in order to be sensitive to its signals and manoeuvre with its activity."

- Simone Jo Moore, SJM

Sales/ buying cycle with dependencies and timelines

Sales cycle or sales process is as much about buying as it is about selling. The two processes will need to be aligned and sales processes have often organically grown to their current state by mirroring customers' procurement processes. Invariably, the process is seen as linear (as below), starting from 'prospect' through to 'paying customer'. On this page, expand the key elements of your sales process. What are the

key stages in the process? Who is involved at which stage? What is your role? Do you have any metrics to track? What are your main goals to achieve during each stage?
(If you work for a futuristic organisation who have embraced a more circular sales process feel free to adapt the diagram accordingly.)

Sales methodologies & meanings

List, circle or draw your favourite sales methodologies, including the one(s) used by your sales team. What can you learn from each methodology? If you could decide, which elements would you keep, leave out, or improve?

Challenger sale

Customer
centric selling

SPIN

M
E
D
D
P
I
C
C

Command of the Message

BANT

Sandler

"I believe sales can be fun. I believe sales can be rewarding."

- Dr Tuuli Bell, author

Client meditation exercise

Meditation is a powerful method to build empathy. In turn, empathy is a key ingredient of emotional intelligence. Emotional intelligence is a human superpower. It sets people apart from cool computers that, though may imitate human behaviour, computers will never create a warm, equitable connection with people. Throughout your career, you'll have built connections with hundreds of people. If it's extra difficult to see another person's perspective, try imagining the person right now. Add your own questions if desired.

Right now, …

...what is your customer thinking?

...what are they talking about?

...what worries them?

...what else is on their mind?

what distracts them?

what do they wear?

...where are they, sitting, standing, walking?

..what do they dream of?

Pick your customer & follow the flow

1. Find a quiet, relaxing space, turn on calming music. {you can try this Amazon Music playlist}

2. Breath in through your nose and breath out through your mouth. Slowly repeat 10 times.

3. Optional: visualise soap bubbles drifting upwards.

4. Open your eyes if they were shut.

5. Go through the questions on the left. Imagine every detail of your customer.

7. As you answer the questions, build a picture of the person; adding text, numbers, or secret symbols.

"Empathy has no script. There is no right way or wrong way to do it. It's simply listening, holding space, withholding judgment, emotionally connecting, and communicating that incredibly healing message of 'You're not alone.'"

- Brené Brown

Opportunity spotting
(getting stuff off my chest)

We all have ideas about what could be improved or fixed. Forgetting about them doesn't solve the problem, and only by changing something will things improve.
Jot down opportunities you've spotted for improving your work. They could include ideas about the product you sell, internal or external-facing processes, tools you use, the way you engage with customers, webinars and conferences you'd like to attend or blog posts you want to write. Use the scale to easily assess the urgency of the idea!

important and...

⟶

..not
urgent

...urgent

(don't bother with unimportant)

29 - my current role

Tracking progress

Spotted opportunity	Benefit(s)	Decision	Done?
Pick your favourite ideas from the chart on the left.	What, why and who does the idea help, is there $$$ attached to it or does it remove a risk?	What, if anything, have I decided to do about the idea?	Time to celebrate life's small wins!

"Should-haves solve nothing. It's the next thing to happen that needs thinking about"

- Alexandra Ripley, Scarlett

My own help guide

This is build-your-own FAQ. You might already have lots of questions to ponder, or just want space to jot down your thoughts right now. If you need inspiration to get started, you could ask yourself: What is stopping me from performing in my role, to the fullest of my ability?

Where do I go to for...
{people, documentation, tools}

Resource & location	Reason for usefulness & who else might benefit

"If you are successful, it is because somewhere, sometime, someone gave you a life or an idea that started you in the right direction. Remember also that you are indebted to life until you help some less fortunate person, just as you were helped."

- Melinda Gates

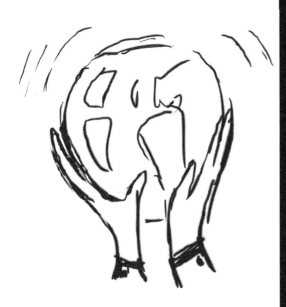

sustainable presales

Sustainability in presales

Presales consultants take pride in being the go-to-experts in many areas: sales, technical matters, and industry trends. So where does sustainability come into play? Domain or industry knowledge requires experience in a certain field (say, banking), but it also requires top presales consultants to stay ahead of the curve in consumer behaviour. And for consumers, sustainability matters.

Sustainability as an underlying principle is still evolving. I feel strongly that sustainability becomes 'real' only once embedded into daily business practices. Sustainable presales is a prime example of adopting sustainability in your organisation. That's also when the magic happens: that's when sustainability brings the aspired business benefits combined with a happier world.

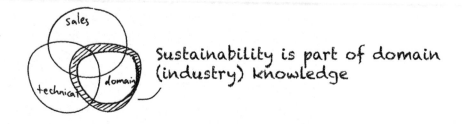

Sustainability is part of domain (industry) knowledge

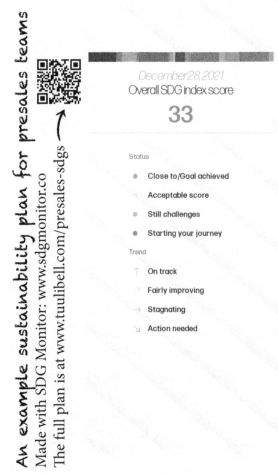

An example sustainability plan for presales teams
Made with SDG Monitor: www.sdgmonitor.co
The full plan is at www.tuulibell.com/presales-sdgs

My SDG Performance
Dashboard

December 28, 2021
Overall SDG index score
33

Status
- Close to/Goal achieved
- Acceptable score
- Still challenges
- Starting your journey

Trend
↑ On track
 Fairly improving
→ Stagnating
↘ Action needed

Volunteer in a local charity	SDG Index: 0 →	
Investments on essential services		
Current date: JAN-2022 Target date: DEC-2022		
Donate profits to local STEM charities	SDG Index: 53 ↑	
Increase of ICT skills		
Current date: MAR-2022 Target date: DEC-2022		
Create a customer case study for climate change use case	SDG Index: 60 ↑	
Increase the sustainable development education		
Current date: FEB-2022 Target date: DEC-2022		
Mentor a colleague or a junior member from another organisation (preferably women)	SDG Index: 44 ↑	
Increase gender equality in leadership and management		
Current date: MAR-2022 Target date: DEC-2023		
Ensure gender balance in leadership	SDG Index: 8	
Increase gender equality & women's empowerment		
Current date: MAR-2022 Target date: MAY-2023		
Share best practice with colleagues	SDG Index: 83 ↑	
Increase domestic resource efficiency		
Current date: JAN-2022 Target date: DEC-2022		
Ensure equal pay within the company	SDG Index: 33	
Increase equal pay for same work		
Current date: MAY-2022 Target date: JUN-2022		
Reduce CO2 footprint of internal	SDG Index:	

#DecadeOfAction

Sustainable business practices will have a positive impact on your business, community and the environment. What are some activities that you can adopt? Can you come up with better ones? Take inspiration from the sustainability plan on the opposite page to get you started.

"One individual cannot possibly make a difference, alone. It is individual efforts, collectively, that makes a noticeable difference——all the difference in the world!"

- Dr Jane Goodall, DBE, primatologist

Going circular

Predominantly, we're living in a so-called linear economy. A linear economy is where an item is sourced from the earth (say, wood), then processed into an item (a coffee cup), used by a consumer (takeaway coffee) and finally thrown in the bin. It's also known as the take, make, use, lose economy.

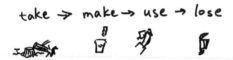

It is evident that linear economy is not sustainable (environmentally or financially). To help re-organise the world's use of resources, circular economy is model that is becoming ever-more mainstream.

Think of the fashion industry, for example, where consumers are financially rewarded for bringing their old clothes back; or the beauty industry where used containers carry a value; or a global furniture chain who will buy your used furniture.

At its core, circular economy re-thinks the product or service that is created and focuses on the outcome using a circular supply chain. I've simplified the idea below: highlighting the blurriness between producer and consumer. The product or service cycle will evolve over time, but essentially you're looking to increase the usage of the product lifecycle (length / intensity / utilisation) and find alternative ways to source the materials. Collection of 'end-of-life' product is a key part of waste management.

The same principles apply to service-only companies, and those selling only digital products.

Circular economy in my industry

How is circular economy embraced in your industry? What are some of the solutions that have been tried by other businesses or communities? Which pilot projects could your company test?

+1 Bonus for those working through the exercise in teams. At the end of the session, go around the room (virtual or physical), and tell the person on your left what you appreciate about them. Feel how the energy of the room is lifted!

"Together and united, we are unstoppable"

- Greta Thunberg, climate activist

Vision of a better future

This is another, lovely, mini art workshop! It works great for both teams and individuals. You can well complete a guided meditation session (see page 28, steps 1-4) first, if you'd like. After finding the right relaxation method for you, continue to the assignment.

Imagine that you live in the future; at a time where everything is perfect. This could be in the near future or years from now. Next, place yourself in that future environment in your place of work. You might work in your current role, or somewhere completely different. Where do you see yourself?

Draw your perfect world of work on these pages as you go through the sensory experience, explored through the questions below.

What do you see around you?

Do you see a creche with children playing nearby? Intergenerational conversation? What do you see in the window, trees, light, the natural world? Or are you perhaps working outdoors?

What do you hear?

Can you hear bird-song? Laughter? Conversations? What do you hear less of? Traffic noise, complaining, devices pinging? Use images, symbols or even colours to describe the auditory experience.

What can you feel?

What do your hands feel when you touch things around you? Can you feel yourself typing on a laptop, or do you do something completely different? Are you mending things with tools, are you creating something?

What do you taste and smell?

What's a dominant smell where you work? Can you smell the freshly made, locally produced lunch? Can you taste something? Are you drinking your favourite drink, or discovered new habits?

What does your heart feel?

Finish your artwork by using colours, shapes or speech bubbles that show how you feel inside. Feel free to play your favourite song, marking the end of the session.

"If we try, we may still fail. But if we do not try, we cannot possibly succeed."
- Christine Milne, former leader of the Australian Greens

career coaching bot

Personality test

Whilst I believe anyone can achieve anything, knowing your personality can act as a catalyst in career path. You can create your own 'shortcuts' by building on your personality's strengths and avoiding common pitfalls. Time to take a fresh personality test? Try this one -->

scan the QR code with your phone. It takes you to

https://www.innerworks.me/

My personality is:

_____

My thoughts about the analysis:

Leveraging your personality in your career

How could you best take advantage of your strengths in your presales career? On the other hand, what are some of the support mechanisms you could take advantage of, to diminish the impact of your weaknesses?

"Doubt is a killer. You just have to know who you are and what you stand for."

- Jennifer Lopez

My path into presales

Draw your path into your current role. What where the life events that led you to this point? Include any important, big or small, moments that have come to define you. Then, re-define what you aspire to be, and continue to draw your path into the future. Include as much detail as you can. What position will you hold? Who will you lead? What industry will you be in? What needs to happen in your personal life in order to support your career development?

What skills do I want to build?

Consider this your candy shop. Circle, draw and write which skills you want to acquire or develop.

Sustainability

Sales

Empathy

Product knowledge

Customer support

Creativity

Customer experience

Software engineering

Industry

"It's possible to climb to the top without stomping on other people."

- Taylor Swift

Who do I need help from?

Who are the mentors, friends, and family that unconditionally love and support me? Are there people that I need that I've yet to meet? Who are they and where can I meet them?

Who do I want to work with?

"It's okay to admit what you don't know. It's okay to ask for help.
And it's more than okay to listen to the people you lead – in fact, it's essential."

- Mary Barra, CEO, General Motors

I am great at presales because

1.   26.

2.   27.

3.   28.

4.   29.

5.   30.

6.   31.

7.   32.

8.   33.

9.   34.

10.   35.

11.   36.

12.   37.

13.   38.

14.   39.

15.   40.

16.   41.

17.   42.

18.   43.

19.   44.

20.   45.

21.   46.

22.   47.

23.   48.

24.   49.

25.   50.

51.   76.

52.   77.

53.   78.

54.   79.

55.   80.

56.   81.

57.   82.

58.   83.

59.   84.

60.   85.

61.   86.

62.   87.

63.   88.

64.   89.

65.   90.

66.   91.

67.   92.

68.   93.

69.   94.

70.   95.

71.   96.

72.   97.

73.   98.

74.   99.

75.   100.

"What you do makes a difference, and you have to decide what kind of difference you want to make."

- Jane Goodall

You made it!

Let's celebrate!!!

Space for mind-clearing

lv

notes

Acronyms

Project Log

Notes, scribbles and doodles

More notes, scribbles and doodles

Dear Presales Champion,

Thank you for choosing this workbook.

I hope you've enjoyed working through the pages as much as I have. Pouring your heart onto paper is not easy but it is very rewarding. I created the workbook to help more people realise their potential. My vision was to create a 'time and space' to think. A journal that provokes thoughts, feelings, and ideas.

In a fast-paced world, we're more connected than ever, yet oddly distant. My dream is that we can all find a community, at home and at work, that supports our individual ambitions. A balanced life that allows each of us to lead fulfilling careers that change the world for the better. You might want to fight cyber criminals from stealing Bitcoins by day and learn Shetland knitting your local community centre by night. Whether I got your passion spot on, or if it's something entirely different, I hope you are now one step closer to achieving your goal.

Have a brilliant day!

Yours faithfully,

Tuuli

Ps. One more request: please help others discover their true calling and leave a review on Amazon today. Thank you!

You might also like

An Introduction to

the Art of

Presales

Dr Tuuli Bell, PhD

An Introduction to the Art of Presales: Breaking the barriers of entry into sales engineering through empathy, creativity and change

https://www.amazon.co.uk/dp/B094XKS2YN

Printed in Great Britain
by Amazon

45338708R00046